Praise for

Insight Selling—Sell Value & Differentiate Your Product
With Insight Scenarios

"In 18-months, our pipeline tripled. Thanks largely to the improved conversations with clients by applying the principals in this book."

Gord Smith, Director of Sales - Hitachi Canada.

"Insight Scenarios are critical to selling value in today's customer-centric economy. This book delivers on how to challenge our customers thinking without challenging the customer – which helps us deliver an exceptional customer experience."

**Jeff Everton, Sales Enablement and Productivity -
Epicor Software**

"Michael has done an outstanding job of providing not only the rationale but also practical ideas on winning in complex sales scenarios. Insight Selling is a blueprint for excelling in a world where we are increasingly seeing the commoditization of sales. The techniques in this book work - I use them every day to help sellers create interest with their prospects and customers, position unique benefits and unexpected sources of value, and create a sense of urgency to act. I highly recommend this book. "

**Anthony Wallace, Dir. Sales Readiness &
Channel Execution APJ - CA Technologies**

INSIGHT SELLING

Sell Value & Differentiate Your Product
With Insight Scenarios

MICHAEL HARRIS

Insight Selling—
Sell Value & Differentiate Your Product With Insight Scenarios

Copyright © 2014 by Michael Harris

Sales & Marketing Press

Printed in Canada

Book Design by Jake Muelle

ISBN 978-0-9936555-0-0

CONTENTS

INTRODUCTION

Selling value to B2B buyers today can feel like trying to stop a freight train that's hurtling towards the sales graveyard of commoditization and discounting. Today, an empowered buyer has done research, has a clear idea of his or her firm's needs, and how much the firm is willing to pay. This type of buyer does not want a salesperson to talk about features and deliver a series of open-ended questions that delivers no value. What this buyer wants is insight. So, how does a salesperson deliver insight so that it challenges the customer's thinking without challenging the customer?

That's the question that this book will answer.

In Part One of this book, we will examine why "Insight Selling" will help you sell value and differentiate your product to empowered buyers.

In Part Two, we will provide six reasons why Insight Scenarios™ trump verbal persuasion at delivering insight to your customers. These reasons are backed by solid research: eight neuroscience studies and 20 research footnotes. The research is then followed by social proof on how SAP, Microsoft & Oracle are doing it.

Finally, in Part Three, we will show you how to create Insight Scenarios, so that you can not only arm your salespeople with insights, but so that you can also show them the most effective way to deliver them.

Once you have created your own insight scenarios, your salespeople will be more effective in two ways:

1. They will be able to deliver insights without upsetting the buyer, and;
2. They will be able to let the customer take your product out for a virtual test drive, so customers will discover for themselves the unique value of your product.

Part One

Why Insight Selling

CHAPTER ONE

INSIGHT SELLING

Complex selling has changed, because buying has changed. In the past, buyers had to approach sellers early in the sales process, because salespeople held the keys to the information kingdom. Today, however, the days of the walking brochure salesman are dead. With the proliferation of information and advice on the Internet, buyers no longer need information from salespeople. What they need is insight. According to recent research, buyers are now 60% of the way through a sales cycle before they engage a salesperson. Why? Because they prefer to do their own research on-line.[1]

In simple sales, these empowered buyers now approach sellers with a clear buying vision of their needs, the solution they want, and what they are willing to pay.

---

[1]   A Corporate Executive Board (CEB) study of more than 1,400 B2B customers across industries revealed that 57% of a typical purchase decision is made before customer even talks to a supplier.

Because they are able to form an accurate buying vision on their own, these buyers can be successful at buying the right solution.

In complex sales, however, this new buying paradigm is often not successful for either the buyer or the seller. Buyers are not successful because they do not have the time or expertise to form an accurate buying vision on their own. They find it difficult, for example, to figure out how the generic value of the seller's product will apply to their specific business and job function. With a limited understanding of the value of the seller's product, buyers either decide not to buy and live with the problem, or they buy on price, ending up with a suboptimal solution. Similarly, sellers are not successful because they achieve lower win rates and reduced margins.

To better understand how the Internet has changed complex sales, just ask yourself what you do when you are a buyer of health care? When you get sick, for instance, do you go onto WebMD before you visit the Doctor? And when you show up at the doctor's office, do you not want him to just write you a prescription for what you feel you need? If the market for buying prescription medicine was truly competitive, would you not also be looking for a better price? Your customers do the same thing before they speak with a salesperson.

Now, if customers and patients could go on-line and buy the right solution, they would not need experts. Doctors and salespeople will tell you, however, that customers and patients do not make good decisions on their own. Imagine a doctor, for example, asking a patient, "what's wrong?" And the patient says, "I was bitten by a mosquito, and with the West Nile virus in the area, I'm concerned. According to WebMD, I believe that I have the identical symptoms, and the recommended treatment is penicillin." "I see," says the doctor, "let me write you a prescription right away." Of course, this would never happen. The doctor's job is not to provide patients with what they think they need. Doctors must provide the optimal solution, and this often requires doctors to challenge their patients' self-diagnoses. Doctors, for instance, have to re-teach what their patients have learned on-line so that their patients end up with the right treatment.

It is the same with complex sales. Today, buyers are more empowered. They use the Internet and social media to research opportunities, and potential solutions. Once they are armed with this information, they attempt to self-diagnose and prescribe. But with the wealth of information available, buyers quickly become flooded by too much information. Once overwhelmed, buyers tend to underestimate the cost of their current behavior, or the potential of future alternatives. With these challenges, it is not surprising that these empowered buyers form an inaccurate buying vision.

So, if salespeople want to sell value and differentiate their product, they have to deliver insight that will reframe the buying vision so buyers end up with the solution that helps them overcome their challenges and achieve their goals.

But how do salespeople do this?

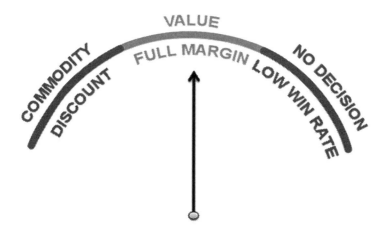

Reframe the buying vision with insight

Figure 1. Insight selling model

By adjusting what we call the three insight dials of contrast, listening, and clarity, we will show in this book how salespeople can reframe the customers' buying vision so that it more accurately reflects their current situation.

1. **Contrast:** Through the use of insight scenarios, the seller is able to increase the contrast between the "before" and "after" pictures associated with owning the seller's product. As sellers increase the

contrast, they increase the value of their product. Think of the before and after photos exercise vendors use.

2. **Listening:** Because the buying vision is like a movie that plays in the buyer's head, the only way a seller can see this image is to listen.

3. **Clarity:** After buyers have shared an image of the before and after picture, sellers can then ask questions to help the buyers to tailor this picture to their particular business and job function.

When the customer's buying vision becomes crystal clear, it is almost as if it becomes a buying simulator® that the buyer can step into so that they are able to take your product out for a virtual test drive. As a result, buyers do not merely think your product is right, but for them, it also feels right because they've been able to internalize why your product is the right fit for their needs.

Leading to Value versus Leading With

In simple sales, salespeople can make sales by leading with their value proposition, because customers are able to form an accurate buying vision on their own.

In complex sales, however, salespeople cannot lead with their value proposition, because the buyer has neither the time nor the expertise to figure out how the seller's generic value will apply to the buyer's specific business and job function. If a salesperson leads the buyer to their value proposition, then the buyer is able to discover the value of the salesperson's product on their own terms.

Historically, sellers have tried to do this by asking questions that lead customers to the type of problems that the sellers' value propositions solve. With the right questions, the belief is that customers will be able to understand the problems that they need to solve and the solutions that are required to solve them.

The problem with this approach is that it assumes that the answers are there within the buyer waiting to be unlocked through the salesperson's questioning skills. By analogy, however, without a doctor's insights, would not a patient question the value that the doctor adds when patients can do this today on-line through sites like WebMD? Likewise, without a salesperson's insights, would not customers question the value that the seller adds when the questions the salesperson asks are no more valuable than what the customers can discover on-line?

If your product helps the buyer to do something new, for instance, how can this buyer answer your questions without a frame of reference? Thus, in complex sales, customers do not want a salesperson to "show up and throw up," and talk about features and benefits. They also do not want the salesperson to show up and deliver a series of open ended questions, death by interrogation, because that also offers no value. What the buyer wants is for the salesperson to be able to deliver insight that will help the buyer form an accurate buying vision.

In conclusion, by not leading the buyer to the seller's value propositions with insights, the seller will experience compressed margins or low win rates, and the buyer will, at best, receive a watered down solution.

What are insights?

When Insight Sellers deliver insights, they shock customers by breaking the customers' thought patterns, and then they rescue customers by replacing the broken pattern with one that is new and improved. That is the "Aha!" experience, and this is how a salesperson reframes the customer's buying vision.

The reason why breaking the customer's thought pattern is so effective at re-framing the customer's thinking is that it is hard wired into our DNA. Our survival has depended on it. Imagine, for example, if Lucy, a hominid living three million years ago on the plains of Africa mistakenly sees a tiger in the grass and runs for cover. No big loss, right? Imagine, however, that she failed to see the pattern of the tiger until it was too late. What happens? She is taken out of the gene pool. So, our survival is contingent on correctly identifying patterns. We are always seeking the meaning that underlies patterns, because uncertainty and chaos terrifies us. Thus, when we see a new pattern, we tell ourselves a cause and effect story to try to predict its outcome so that it cannot hurt us. But when we see an established pattern, we discount it as common sense, because without such a filter, we would drown in information.

The response a salesperson is looking for from the customer when they deliver insight is not "Yes, that's exactly what I was thinking," because this would mean that the salesperson had not broken the customer's thought pattern. The response the salesperson seeks is "Hmm, I had not considered that," because we're wired to not ignore new patterns.

By delivering insights that expands the customer's thinking, the customer will start to tell themselves a new story where new choices makes more sense. To reframe the customer's thinking, however, the salesperson must have insight to deliver. So how do you find and create insight?

Finding insights

Salespeople find insight by figuring out what is counterintuitive about their core sales message? Where is the gap between what the customer believes today, and what they need to believe to buy your product?

A marketing company, for example, could present its client with research that shows that B2B companies on average win 24% of sales opportunities, lose 16% to their competition, and see 60% of sales opportunities lost to a no decision outcome. Based on this research, the marketing company could reframe its client's thinking that their greatest competition comes not from another company, but rather from customers who have decided not to buy. With this insight, the marketing company could help improve their customer's marketing message by focussing more on "why change" instead of just showing "why us."

Unfortunately, you may discover that you find insight only a small percent of the time. Most of the time, you will have to work at trying to create insights.

Creating Insights

We suggest you try to create insight by simply increasing the contrast between hell if the customer remains with their current broken pattern, and heaven if they adopt your new and improved pattern. Then ask questions to help the customer fill in the picture with personal details so that the customer's image has achieved clarity with respect to the customer's title/job function and company.

With this approach, you are betting that the customer does not yet have the insight to see this image at its maximum contrast and clarity. This is generally a good bet, because customers lack both the time and expertise to see this image on their own. As a result, the customer's buying vision is narrow and vague.

This approach is also a good bet because other salespeople are often only able to paint a superficial picture of the problem, for example, the customer's current system is prone to error or lacks timeliness. Because they lack the knowledge of the customer needed to help the customer complete the picture, the salesperson is unable to help improve the buying vision. This in turn means that the buyer will see little value in the seller's product.

According to a recent McKinsey report, "While insight conjures up visions of research, data crunching, and "aha" moments, real strategic insight also rests on a seemingly mundane and easy-to-overlook factor: a thorough understanding of how and why a company, its competitors, and others in the industry value chain make money. Absent dumb luck, a strategy that does not tap directly into such an understanding will under-perform.[2]"

---

[2] McKinsey Insights & Publications, "Mastering the building blocks of strategy," Oct 13, 2013.

A salesperson has to be sure, however, not to provide "free consulting," and then have the customer buy the product cheaper from a competitor. To avoid free consulting, the salesperson has to try to insert a few unique capabilities into the insights that they deliver.

Delivering Insights Can Be Difficult

We may think it is easy for a doctor to challenge what a patient may learn online, but a family doctor recently complained to me how patients come into her office demanding antibiotics because they have gone onto WebMD and became convinced they have an infection. Even though she is wearing the white coat and the stethoscope, she is generally not successful at convincing them that they just have a virus.

Another friend of mine is a chiropractor, and he laments: "In the time it takes to drive to my clinic, my patients could have done the exercises at home that I recommended. But instead, they show-up at my clinic, and insist on an adjustment."

So, in both cases, the patients did not want to do the work to heal themselves, because they would rather get the magic quick fix of a pill or an adjustment.

Are customers any different? Constrained by time and expertise, do customers want to do the work needed to fully diagnose their problem, and then appreciate all of the suppliers' unique capabilities so that they can then decide on the optimal solution? Or will they become overwhelmed, and then boil everything down to the lowest common denominator, and buy on price?

If doctors struggle to reframe their patients' thinking, imagine how hard it is to reframe a high powered executive's thinking, especially when you have "salesperson" written on your business card?

So how can a salesperson challenge the customer's thinking, without challenging the customer?

If you thought that Insight Selling was simply using data, facts, and your brilliance to shock and awe buyers about the errors of their ways, then you may want to rethink this approach, because how you deliver the insight will determine if you are perceived as provocative or arrogant.

There are four ways to challenge customers with insights, but we will show that insight scenarios are the best way to deliver insights.

1. **Directly:** This can come across as an attack. Since the customer is both judge and jury, this is an argument that the salesperson will rarely win. Under such circumstances, the customer may feel attacked, become defensive, and shut down.
2. **Questions:** They work best at firming up an established belief. It is difficult, however, to lead customers to insights with questions, because they have no frame of reference that they can turn to for the answers.
3. **Research:** Because research is objective, customers do not usually feel attacked. Unfortunately, research is scarce and seldom available.
4. **Insight Scenario:** Because an insight scenario is about someone else, the customer does not feel

attacked. It simply presents a scenario that allows the customer to draw their own conclusions. Without feeling pressured, the customer can now relax and listen to your story, and possibly gain enough insight to start telling themselves a new story, where new choices make more sense.

So through a combination of insight scenarios, listening, and questions, we will show how salespeople can effectively deliver insights that will reframe their customer's buying vision, so that they can sell value and differentiate their product.

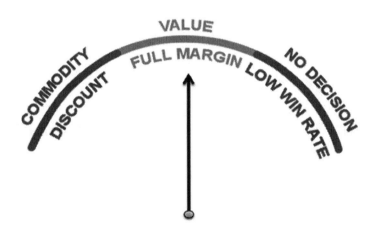

Reframe the buying vision with insight

Contrast	**Listening**	**Clarity**
with	for	with
Insight Scenarios	Buying Vision	Questions

Figure 2. Insight Selling model

Chapter Two

INSIGHT SCENARIOS

We believe insight scenarios are the best tool that your salespeople can use to sell value and differentiate their product. To support this claim, we present you with six reasons why insight scenarios are the best way, and later in the book, we will explore these reasons in greater detail.

Six Benefits

1. Puts the customer's ego to sleep

With an insight scenario, you can deliver insights that will only challenge the customer's thinking, and not the customer. Because insight scenarios are about someone else, the customer does not feel under attack. A story simply presents a scenario that allows the customer to draw their own conclusions. Without feeling pressured, the customer can now relax and listen to your message, and possibly gain enough insight that they start to tell themselves a new story, where new choices make more sense.

2. Makes the customer care

Facts and figures are too abstract. You cannot see them or feel them, so they do not feel like they affect you either directly or indirectly. Without context, the customer is left to try to figure out why it makes sense to buy, or worse, why they should care.

3. Generates Value

Before your salespeople can close the value gap for your product, they first have to open it. An Insight Scenario does this by providing a clear word picture of what the buyer's circumstances are before ownership, and what they are after ownership. Because customers generally discount claims for gains, the salesperson must help the customer to realize that they are not ankle deep in problems, but that they're really drowning in the middle of the lake before the customer is ready to see the value of being rescued by your product.

4. Memorable

A fact, wrapped in an emotional Insight Scenario story, is 20 times more memorable than the same fact presented simply as a matter of fact.[3] Even if a salesperson persuades a customer how great their offering is with facts, they only did so on an intellectual basis, and buyers are not inspired to act on reason alone. To drive through a buying cycle, the

---

[3] Jerome Bruner, cognitive psychologist.

customer needs not only logic as the steering wheel, but also emotion as the gas pedal.

5. Hard wired into our DNA

Humans have told Insight Scenario stories visually for 100,000 years, orally for 10,000 years, and in writing for 6,000 years. All the way back to early man, stories were the technology that we used to share information vital to our survival. Early man, for example, might have said, "You better not eat those berries, because John, your uncle, ate them, and here's what happened..."

6. Sharpens the saw

Insight Scenario sales coaching will allow you to find and fill the customer knowledge gaps in your sales team. Because an insight scenario presents a clear before and after picture of owning your product, knowledge gaps are immediately exposed when the picture is out of focus.

Case studies

You may be wondering, "I already have case studies, so why do I need to go to the trouble of creating insight scenarios?"

We would agree that once a buyer has formed their buying vision, case studies are a great tool to use late in the sales cycle as proof and reinforcement. Early in a sales cycle, however, case studies are not effective at helping customers to reframe their buying vision for the following three reasons: 1) case studies are conversation-killing monologues that floods the customer with too much information; 2) they focus too much on product proof, and not enough on selling the problem before the solution, and; 3) they are too generic to deliver insight.

Example

Here's an example of an insight scenario that an advanced planning software salesperson could share with the CFO of a customer to provide insight on what is needed for orders to be truly profitable.

Maxine, the Supply Chain Director of Asahi Glass, wanted a way to know what orders were truly profitable.

Up until now, the salespeople had been using a static snapshot of profitability.

Maxine, however, was disappointed to see profitable deals later become money losers. This occurred because the salespeople would place orders with no insight into how they impacted current capacity, nor if their rush orders would negatively impact other orders.

Maxine needed to find a way to have a more dynamic view of profitability, something that was simple for the salespeople to use. What she envisioned was something as simple as booking a flight on-line, with a number of scheduling options according to price for the customer, and true profitability for Maxine's company.

Maxine finally had enough when a salesperson's profitable Toyota order quickly turned into a substantial money loser because her company was forced to fly parts into the plant to avoid delayed order penalties.

Fortunately, the Toyota order inspired Maxine to look for a solution, and she found more than what she was looking for with Advance Schedule Corp.

We provided Maxine with the ability to see each potential order's impact on capacity, and then how it affected other orders.

The sales team was elated that they could now do sales campaigns by pooling their orders along with price incentives so that they could not just generate more sales, but more importantly, maintain profitability.

But that's Maxine's story, what's yours?

CHAPTER THREE

INSIGHT SELLING IN ACTION

Now that we've looked at what insight selling is and why it is effective, it is now time to look at how you would use insight selling in a client meeting. Please note that these steps are sales methodology neutral.

A Seven-Step Approach:

1. Value assumption

After initial introductions, a salesperson can start the meeting off by sharing three to five value hypotheses to initiate a discussion.

This approach came about through a conversation with a customer. A few years ago, a customer mentioned that buyers no longer seemed eager to answer 20 questions so that they could teach the salesperson how to sell them their product. Just like customers do not want people to "show up and throw up," they also no longer wanted death by interrogation where a salesperson asks them a series of manipulative questions.

The customer said that he'd recently worked with McKinsey, and he was intrigued how they started each meeting with hypothesis-based selling. I asked, "Do they provided a laundry list of business pains, and then have the customer choose their most pressing critical business issue." He said: "No, because if you're just selling to known business issues, then you're not providing insight. You've got to be bold, Michael. Because you're presenting value assumptions that may be hidden, your customers may not be able to pick a business pain, or even fully appreciate that they have one."

So that is how we started mining for hidden value. Based on similar customers and pre-meeting research, we would start each meeting with three to five value assumptions/ hypotheses. This would often lead into a 10-minute high-level dialogue with the buyer. While discussing the value assumptions, this was also an excellent time to bring up benchmark data, or information the salesperson had uncovered through their pre-call research.

2. Listening for hidden value

During this conversation, the salesperson would be listening for gaps between the ideal buying vision and the current buying vision. This would ensure that the salesperson could focus for the rest of the meeting on a value the customer had not yet fully recognized.

3. Increase contrast with insight scenarios

The salesperson will not directly present the value gap. Trying to convince customers that they have a problem often leads to an argument that the salesperson rarely wins. The last thing, for example, that an overwhelmed buyer needs is another salesperson's solution looking for a problem. Instead, the salesperson will share a short insight scenario (250-350 words) that takes no longer than 90-120 seconds to deliver. This insight-based story approach removes the one thing customers hate most from being in the company of salespeople, namely, the feeling of being pressured. Without the pressure, the buyer can relax, and, if the story is insightful and one that they can see themselves in, the buyer may start to tell themselves a new story where new choices make more sense. So, show, and do not tell. Let the buyer convince themselves, and in turn, take ownership of the problem.

Figure 3. Traditional Selling vs. Insight Selling

To make your insight scenarios stickier, you may wish to present a clear before and after drawing (see figure 3). The before picture should show all of the problems and costs to your buyer's business operations in the absence of having the unique capabilities of your product, and the after drawing will show how they used your offering to solve their problem. By increasing the contrast between the before and after picture, you have increased the delta (i.e., value) of your product. Also, 72 hours after you leave the customer's office, a customer remembers only 10% of the spoken word, but will remember 65% if the spoken word is accompanied by a picture.[4] So, insight scenarios are memorable, because they are word pictures. In workshops, I have also seen how these pictures really help salespeople become clear in articulating value.

4. Listen for clarity

A salesperson only shares an insight scenario with the buyer so that the buyer will reciprocate with the buyer's story. The insight scenario helps the buyer find the "oil spills" in the buyer's own company. If the buying vision is big and clear, it's time for the salesperson to start discussing the solution with the buyer.

5. Increase clarity with questions

If the buying vision is not clear, the salesperson can follow up with a few questions to help the customer fill in the details so that the seller's generic value can become specific to the buyer.

6. Solution

Hopefully by now, the buyer has bought into the concept of your product, and all that you need to do now is

---

[4]   Brain Rules, Dr. John Medina, 2008, p. 234

present your solution. If needed, you can offer a few proof points to help the buyer to justify their decision to buy.

7. Echo letter

The salesperson may then follow-up on the meeting with a letter that articulates the reframed buying vision. This letter will not only confirm the salesperson's understanding of the new buying vision, but it may also be used by the buyer to sell access to other key players behind closed doors. The salesperson may then meet with the other key players, and reframe the buying vision for the company.

So, there you have it. Instead of selling blind and trying to sell value, the salesperson can present a few value assumptions, discover the hidden value, and then fill in the value gaps with insight scenarios, listening, and questions.

Stages	Provoke	Engage	Consult	Evaluate	Close
Inputs	• Maximum Credibility Proposal	Conversation 1. Deliver insight: Insight Scenario 2. Develop insight: listen & ask questions	• Access to other Key Player(s) • Key Player Echo Letters	• Potential Value Proposal	• Negotiate
Outputs	•Net New Mtg.	Echo Letter	Access "Qualified Opportunity"	Evaluation Plan	Win/Loss
Measure	(1) Track Sales Funnel	(2) Track Sales Funnel	(3) 25% Sales Forecast	(4) 50% Sales Forecast	(5) 90% Verbal Sales Forecast

Figure 4. Suggested sales process

CHAPTER FOUR

SOCIAL PROOF

With the rise of the empowered buyer, it is no wonder that the three largest software companies Microsoft, Oracle, and SAP have embraced insight selling. But these companies have also learned that there is a gap between theory and the practical application, because insight selling is more than just using data, facts, and brilliance to shock and awe buyers about the error of their ways.

These companies have discovered that how their sales force delivers insight will determine if they are perceived as provocative or arrogant, and more importantly, if their insight is successful at reframing the buying vision. We believe that the best way to deliver insight is to wrap the insight inside an insight scenario-a unique form of business storytelling.

It would appear that the top software companies agree as SAP and Microsoft, for instance, have hired Chief Storytellers.[5] Before we look into how SAP and Oracle are

---

[5]   Julie Roehm, SAP, and Steve Clayton, Microsoft.

using stories to deliver insights, let us first do a thought experiment, so that you can discover for yourself which is more likely to inspire you to act, an insight delivered by facts and figures or an insight scenario?

1. Insight scenario

Imagine you are the VP of Sales for Software USA. After an overnight flight, you are walking over the Waterloo Bridge in London on a sunny April morning. You are on your way to the biggest interview of your life- to run your European operations.

After investing over $1,000 on a new wardrobe for this very important interview, you sidestep a puddle, to avoid getting your new shoes wet. Just then, out of the corner of your eye, you see a small girl fall off the bridge into the frigid water below. As she cries for help, without thinking, you jump in to rescue her.

As you emerge from the river, you notice that your suit and shoes are ruined. But that's quickly forgotten, when you look down into the frightened girl's eyes, and realize that she is just about the same age as your daughter.

2. Facts & figures scenario

The next day, after a successful but wet interview, you are flipping through the Economist magazine in the hotel bar. As you finish your drink, you notice an advertisement for relief victims of the Indonesian Tsunami. For a fraction of the cost of your ruined wardrobe, you are informed how your contribution could save hundreds of people. There are plenty of facts and figures about airlifts of medicine, medical supplies, and water purification. But the facts do not grab you, and you are quickly flooded with too much information. You disengage, look at your watch, and decide it is time to leave for the airport.

Concrete stories trump abstract facts

If you are like most people, one personalized story about a girl on a bridge has infinitely more impact than the impersonalized generalization in The Economist, even if the impact of the generalization is 100 times greater. Studies have shown that charities sending out donation letters, for example, pull twice the donations when the letter is about one person as opposed to the presentation of facts and figures about many.[6]

SAP story

When the world's largest business software company, for example, hires a Chief Storyteller, it is news, because this is an industry first.

And when the decision was made by SAP's CEO, Bill McDermott, it became a great story.

- Why, for instance, did Bill feel that the role of Chief Storyteller was so important that he personally recruited Julie Roehm 18 months ago for the role?

---

[6] Small D., Lowenstein G., & Slovic P. "Can Insight Breed Callousness? The Impact of Learning about Identifiable Victim Effect on Sympathy," Working Paper University of Pennsylvania, 2005.

- Why did he hire a B2C candidate for a B2B role?
- Given all of Bill's experience (Sales Xerox, President Gartner, Exec VP of Worldwide Sales & Operations Siebel, and CEO SAP), what insights can we gain from his decision?

Bill wanted Julie and her team of 90-employees to be the proof point for SAP's work. For the proof to stick, Bill felt that he needed someone from B2C who was able to wrap SAP's facts up in emotion to form a story. Because even if a salesperson persuades a customer how great an offering is with facts, Bill knew that buyers are not inspired to act on reason alone. To buy, the customer must not only think an offering is right, but more important, the customer must feel that it is right. Rated as one of the 100 leading women in the North American Auto Industry by Automotive News, Julie was the perfect fit, because cars are primarily an emotional sale.

So what happens if you do not wrap up your facts in emotion to form a story? Well, if your salespeople do not introduce the main buying themes with a quick two-minute story, will they not sound as if they are reading straight from a product manual? Without a story to give your product context, how can your customers arrive at a buying decision, or even care?

If your salespeople are merely claiming that your product can improve results by 20%, do they not sound like every other software vendor? Will the prospect not discount those claims by 90%?

On the other hand, what would happen if they instead shared a story about a similar customer, a story that highlighted in detail the limitations of this similar customer's current system? Would the prospect not suddenly see how the prospect's system could potentially be improved? Would prospects then be more willing to hear about your solution, because your salesperson first sold the problem? Would you not agree that you've got to open the gap before you can close it?

Ask yourself whether, if your salespeople shared just one story per meeting, and did everything else the same, would customers relate more to what your salespeople are selling? Would you sell more?

Oracle story

John Burke, Group Vice President, Oracle Corporation shares his story on the importance of using insight scenarios.

> Throughout our careers, we have been trained to ask diagnostic questions, deliver value props, and conduct ROI studies. It usually doesn't work; best case, we can argue with the customer about numbers—purely a left brain exercise, which turns buyers off.... Large companies are often very adept at explaining what their products do, but not as adept at explaining how and why their customers use their products. Most companies, Oracle included, have made a great effort to become more customer-focused, and there have been a lot of sales training programs put into place to accomplish that. However, I've observed over the years that many of those programs

don't seem to help much, because salespeople don't often know the real stories behind why their customers bought and how their customers actually use their products.[7]

Al Gore zero to hero

Irrespective of your political beliefs, I am sure you will agree that the change in Al Gore, once he learned the power of storytelling, was nothing short of striking. You may remember in 1999 that the Washington Post published a poll that concluded that 56% of the American public describe the vice-president as "very boring" or "somewhat boring." Being described as boring for a politician is the equivalent of a salesperson on their last improvement plan. But when Al learned to tell a story with the "An Inconvenient Truth" presentation, he won an Emmy, an Oscar, and a Nobel Peace Prize. So, imagine if insight scenarios could do for your salespeople what they did for Al Gore?

But we already tell stories

You think that your sales team is already effective at sharing insightful stories with customers? Well, here's a quick way to check:

- Write down the three biggest gaps between what your prospective customers believe, and what they need to believe to buy your product.

---

[7] How Oracle Uses Storytelling to Sell More, cbsnews.com, April, 2011.

- Pick one, and ask a few random salespeople what story they would tell to bridge this gap?
- Do not give them time to prepare. Customers are impatient, so they will not have time to develop their story in front of a customer.
- Tell them that if they lapse into explaining what your product does, then they have failed, because they will have flooded the customer with too much information.

The good news is that this information is already in your sales force, because a few members of your sales team are exceeding quota. And if you can zero in on what are the insight scenarios that your top performers tell, you can then put them into a consistent format. The rest of your team will then have the magic sauce to inspire your customers to buy.

Even if members of your team do not deliver these customer insights as stories, but instead through customer conversations, the story format is a simple way to package this information, since stories are easy to recall in the heat of a sales call. In fact, according to Jerome Bruner, a cognitive psychologist, a fact wrapped in a story is 22 times more memorable than one that is not.

Because these insight scenarios are made by salespeople for salespeople, your team members will not feel that you are imposing just another sales methodology on them. In fact, unlike other sales training programs that become shelf ware, your salespeople can use the stories created in this manner the very next day with customers.

CHAPTER FIVE

INSIGHT SELLING CHALLENGES

A ll sellers want their salespeople to be trusted advisers. This is especially true today, now that salespeople no longer hold the keys they once did to the information kingdom. Today, to add value, salespeople must do more than just provide information; they need to provide *insight*. For salespeople to become insight sellers, they must overcome two fundamental challenges.

1- Customer knowledge

The first challenge is acquiring enough knowledge about the customer to provide the basis for insight. In the ideal world, the best way to sell a product is for the buyer to use it for six months first, because they will then discover the value of the product on their terms. The second best way to sell the product is for your salespeople to have previously worked in customer service. They can then share with buyers the insights that they gained as they saw how other customers used the product. Of course, the only problem with this approach is that it's expensive sales training. The third approach is for your top customer service and salespeople to share their insights with the rest of your team through insight scenarios.

You may, however, feel that it's a waste of time for your sales team to acquire customer knowledge as their time is better spent selling. If that's the case, let me share with you a story, and you may see things differently afterwards. I can remember once asking for more details on how a customer could use our product, and Tim, our Managing Director, joked: "Michael, you're in sales, you're too stupid to understand." The sad thing was that this was what he, and his delivery team, really believed. And when I wanted customer stories from marketing, I only got the watered down versions, because marketing did not trust sales to use these stories with customers. The marketing people had the executive team sand off the rough corners that made the stories interesting- to the point that they were useless.

So there I was standing outside the walls of customer knowledge, trying to prepare for a potential customer meeting with the few scraps of information management decided to throw down to sales. And when I left for these meetings, I had all the confidence of a soldier rushing a machine gun bunker armed with blanks. I knew that the customer would be able to poke a finger through my knowledge, because it was paper thin. The fact that many of my competitors were in the same position did not help, because the customers generally chose not to buy from either of us.

Fortunately this nightmare came to an end when I became best friends with Lee, an ambitious member of the delivery team. We were both strong where the other was weak. He had the technical and customer knowledge, and I had the sales knowledge. So Lee came to my meetings to learn the front-end of the business, and I went to his meetings to learn the back-end of the business. Although we were not required to attend each other's meetings, we viewed this time as a long-term investment in our professional development.

Boy, did that investment pay off. Sure customers still tried to poke holes in our knowledge, but they quickly discovered it was a mile deep. Where other salesmen would flinch, we were as solid as steel, because we were confident that we were leading the customer down the right path.

News of our success spread, and pretty soon I was hired by the competition to run their European office. Naturally, I took Lee with me. We increased sales seven times, and in so doing doubled the size of our previous company. And Tim, our old boss, lost his job, because he foolishly thought that his salespeople were too stupid to understand.

So do not underestimate your salespeople. They are smart and ambitious.

The good news is that you already possess plenty of information on your customers. After all, a few members of your sales team are exceeding quota.

Don't worry, your salespeople do not have to know more about the buyers' businesses than they know themselves. However, they must know the problems and costs to your customers' operations in the absence of having your unique capabilities.

Unfortunately, a great deal of marketing collateral does not provide the customer knowledge needed by sales to help buyers decide to change from the status quo. In fact, most material is geared towards "Why You?" that is, why the seller's product is the most cost-effective, low risk, and high-value solution. But before buyers can appreciate "Why You?" they first have to answer "Why Change?" and "Why Now?" For buyers to appreciate being rescued by your product, they have to feel as though they are out in the middle of the Lake, drowning in problems. If the seller continues to lead with "Why us?" instead of "Why Change?" then salespeople will be selling to Buyers who feel they are only ankle deep in problems, and they will not appreciate the need for the salesperson's product. This explains why so many B2B sales opportunities stall in the pipeline. According to a recent survey by Sales Benchmark Index, over 60% of sales opportunities end with the buyer deciding to stick with the status quo, and not buying.

In addition to helping the buyer to understand "Why Change?" your sales force also needs to get crystal clear on what are your company's unique differentiators; otherwise, they will risk merely offering free consulting. Unfortunately, if you ask 10 people from marketing and sales what your company does better than anyone else, you will most likely get 10 different answers.

It would be a shame, for instance, for your salesperson to motivate the customer to act without inserting at least one key differentiator into the buyer's decision criteria, only to then have the customer put this new buying vision out to bid. Therefore, to avoid giving away free consulting, it's important for your salespeople to understand and deliver,

"Why would a customer buy from you rather than from someone else?"

As we stated earlier, the good news is that this information is already within your company, because your top customer service and salespeople are achieving superior results. You can also augment this information by conducting customer interviews.

2- Delivery

Sellers want their salespeople to be provocative, but this must be achieved in a consultative way; otherwise, the salesperson may be viewed as arrogant, or even worse, confrontational.

If the Achilles' heel of Solution Selling was complexity, then the Achilles' heel of challenging customers with insight is how to challenge the customer's thinking without challenging the customer?

As a result of teaching Solution Selling for five years, I learned the number one complaint of sales managers was that the bottom 80 percent of their salespeople quit trying to use the methodology within 10 days of the workshop, giving, as a reason, that it was too complicated. According to McKinsey, for example, "Solutions Selling has been all the rage over the last 5 to 10 years, yet 75 percent of the companies that attempt to offer solutions fail to return the cost of their investment.[8]"

In the heat of a sales call, Salespeople cannot be expected to remember 50-200 questions, especially

---

[8]   Solution Selling: Is the pain worth the gain' McKinsey Study

when the buyer's response to the salesperson's questions could jump from question 23 to 58 and then back to 17. The Salespeople would get lost in a sea of questions, because the sequential nature of the questioning model was too inflexible to adjust to the fluidity of a business conversation. I did find, however, that the people who helped put together the questions were successful at Solution Selling, because they knew the before and after picture behind the questions. They didn't need to memorize the questions, so they could easily pivot with the buyer. They did, however, have one very important complaint. When they were selling something new to the customer, the customer was often not able to answer their questions, because the customer had no frame of reference. If your software, for example, will require the customer to act in a new way, then the buyer must be able to see how they would use it to improve their business before they are able to answer questions about the deficiency of their current system. Thus, this gap in the flow of the selling dialogue was what led me to insight scenarios, because stories are easier to remember, and they can open the door to new ways of thinking. They are also effective at challenging the customer's thinking without challenging the customer, because they are about someone else and, therefore, nonthreatening.

To ensure that challenging customers with insights does not go the same way of Solution Selling, it's got to be easy for the salesperson to deliver; otherwise, salespeople will simply revert back to their product PowerPoint presentations. Delivering an insight scenario is the way to go, because it is non-confrontation and easy to remember.

Part Two

Why Insight Scenarios

CHAPTER SIX

CONTRAST

B y providing insight, the salesperson is able to reframe the customers' buying vision so that they see a greater contrast between the before and after picture of owning the seller's product. By increasing this contrast, the salesperson increases the product's value.

This value, rarely recognized or developed, exists for two reasons. The first is that the buyer has neither the time nor the expertise to self-diagnose problems and prescribe solutions. To make matters worse, most salespeople are not able to help the customer form an accurate buying vision, because they are selling blind. Without a helicopter view of the customer's world, the salesperson is not able to take a generic value proposition and help the customer discover the value of the product on the customer's own terms. The result is that the buyer will either make a purchase based on price or decide to live with the problem. Customers will buy on price, because they do not recognize the full value of a seller's offering. As a result, all of the suppliers' offerings look the same; thus, the only variable is price. The buyer ends up with a watered down solution without ever understanding the full value of the seller's product, and the seller will experience compressed margins. Alternatively, the buyer's limited view of the seller's product will be overshadowed in the buyer's mind by the risk of change. As a result, the customer will not buy, and will instead decide to live with the problem.

Open before you close the value gap

Before sellers can close the value gap with their product, they first have to open it. The salesperson cannot lead with value, but must instead lead the buyer to the value. I discovered the importance of this lesson a few years ago when the Marketing Director of Eaton Corp asked me to come in and work with five of their verticals to create the value propositions they needed for a global executive conference. In the first meeting, one of their top hydraulics salespeople was sitting at the front of the workshop with his arms crossed. He was managing Waste Management, an account the size of a Third World country's GDP. I figured I better ask what the problem was before I got started. He said, "If you think I'm going to present marketing's value props to my customers, you've got another thing coming." "Why is that?" I asked. He said, "Because my customer will say if I believed every salesperson that said how they were going to reduce my fuel costs by 30%, I'd have my trucks parked out on the street selling gas, instead of hauling garbage." (See figure 5)

Figure 5. Value Proposition vs. Insightful Story

What this salesperson knew was that if the value proposition promised a 30% improvement, the customer would discount 90% of it. So instead of selling the upside, he would reduce the buyer's firm's baseline by showing how it was not doing it well today. Once the buyer could see that the firm was not doing things well, it would be easy to see how results could be improved. Thus, reducing the customer's baseline is a good strategy, because Buyers often overestimate their current position. But it is not just buyers that overestimate their baseline. 90% of people rate themselves as above average drivers. So it is hard to sell a solution to someone who does not feel that they have a problem. That is why it is so important to increase the contrast, because it increases the need for your product.

Research confirms the need for contrast

In a recent Forrester Research report, 75% of salespeople agreed that the most important aspect of a successful meeting with prospective buyers is an ability to understand the buyers' business issues, and share a way to solve them.[9] According to Sirius Decisions, a sales and marketing consultancy, the two biggest inhibitors of sales effectiveness are: 1) the inability to communicate the value message, and 2) subject matter expertise of the industry or solution.[10] These finding are confirmed in a B2B customer survey of executives by Forrester Research, where the researchers found that executives felt that only 12% of sales calls added value.[11]

Contrast needs three things to be effective

Our premise has been that salespeople need customer knowledge and subject matter expertise to enable them to shine a light on the buyer's unrecognized value. And delivering insight will enable the buyer to see greater contrast and, thereby, greater value. To be effective at creating contrast, the message should be packaged in an insight scenario so that it will be: 1) Non-confrontational; 2) concrete, and; 3) wrapped in emotion. This is what we will focus on in the following three chapters.

---

[9] "What Do Reps Believe Makes A Meeting Successful?" Forrester Research, Nov 2013.

[10] Summit 2013 Highlights: How to Conquer the Changing World of B-to-B Buying, Sirius Decisions.

[11] ExecutiveBuyerInsightStudy:AreSalespeoplePreparedForExecutive Conversations? Forrester Research, Aug. 2012.

CHAPTER SEVEN

NON-CONFRONTATIONAL

Because they prefer to do their own research online, many buyers can now be 60% of the way through a sales cycle before they engage a salesperson. These empowered buyers will then contact salespeople with an idea concerning their needs, the solution they want, and what they are willing to pay. So, to sell the value of their product, the salesperson will often have to reframe the customer's buying vision. But reframing the buying vision is a difficult challenge for salespeople for two reasons.

1- Skeptical

The first reason is that customers are inherently skeptical of what salespeople say. In the past, customers have bought into the promises made by salespeople only to discover that they did not materialize. There have been studies, for instance, that over two thirds of CRM (customer relationship management software) or ERP (enterprise resource planning) implementations have not delivered the intended ROI.

2- Confirmation bias

The second reason is that the customer's confirmation bias acts as a wall to opposing views. Just think of your partner asking, "Do these jeans make me look fat?" You may think your partner is looking for the truth, but what your partner is really looking for is reassurance.

The harder the salesman pushes, the more the customer pushes back. Customers push back because of their confirmation bias, and research concludes that strongly held convictions can actually harden in the face of contradictory rational evidence.[12] In 1979, for example, a team at Stanford University ran an interesting study where they measured the strength of the subjects' beliefs on capital punishment. The subjects were then asked to read short research reports for and against capital punishment. You would think that their beliefs would become more balanced after they read an opposing view, but their beliefs actually hardened. The confirmation bias does not just exist for highly emotive beliefs. It's also alive and well in science and among scientists themselves. Scientists, for example, have been found to rate more favorably studies that report findings consistent with their prior beliefs than

---

[12] Lord, C., Ross, L., & Lepper, M. (1979). Biased Assimilation and Attitude Polarization: The Effects of Prior Theories on Subsequently Considered Evidence. *Journal of Personality and Social Psychology*, 37(11), 2098-2109.

studies reporting findings inconsistent with their previous beliefs.[13]

Status quo

So, imagine you are a salesperson, and you are trying to reframe the buying vision of your customer. To do so, your argument has to climb not only a wall of skepticism, but it also has to get past the buyer's confirmation bias. No wonder 60% of sales opportunities end with the buyer deciding not to buy.[14]

Insight Scenario

Instead of trying to win a debate with a customer, a salesperson will succeed more often by putting the rational reasons to buy a product inside a series of insight scenarios, like a Trojan horse, so that your sales message gets past the customer's defensive wall and is more likely to be heard.

With an insight scenario, you can deliver insights that will challenge the customers' thinking, and not the customer. Because insight scenarios are about someone else, customers do not feel like they are being attacked. A story simply presents a scenario that allows customers to

---

[13] Mahoney, Michael J. (1977). Publication prejudices: an experimental study of confirmatory bias in the peer review system., *Cognitive Therapy and Research* 1(2), 161–175.

[14] Sales Benchmark Index's recent survey of over 3,000 B2B companies found that 28% of sales opportunities were won, 12% were lost to the competition, and 58% were lost to no decision.

draw their own conclusions. Without feeling pressured, customers can now relax and listen to your message, and possibly gain enough insight that they will start to tell themselves a new story, where new choices make more sense.

CHAPTER EIGHT

CONCRETE

Many salespeople feel that if they just educate the customer enough, they will buy. But they do not, because without context, the buyer does not know why they should buy, or even worse, why they should care. So why do salespeople not add context so that buyers are able to connect the dots between the salesperson's offering, and their business and job function?

Context makes your message concrete

There are two reasons why it's difficult for salespeople to add context so that their sales message will be concrete. The first is that it's scary for a salesperson to sit across the table from a C-level executive, and have a business conversation. The C-level executive may have 20 years of deep industry experience, and the salesperson may have only a couple of years of product knowledge, and whatever industry knowledge the salesperson could pick up in the process. Salespeople in this situation feel as if they are swimming in a sea of uncertainty, and that's why they cling to the security of the product PowerPoint presentation. That's what they know, and that's what they revert back to when they hit a bump in the road, such as trying a new consultative sales approach.

The second reason salespeople do not provide the needed context is the curse of knowledge. The curse of knowledge happens when you ask an expert a question, and get back an answer that sounds as if it were in another language. Think back to the last time you asked a lawyer a simple question. Even though you received a perfectly good legal answer, you did not understand a word he was saying. An excellent study that explains why experts suffer from the curse of knowledge took place at Stanford University in 1990. In the study, the subjects were split into two groups of "the tappers" and "the listeners." The tappers were asked to tap one of 25 well-known songs, and the listeners were tasked to guess the song based on the rhythm being tapped. However, before the researchers asked the listener the name of the song, they asked the tapper what they thought the probability was that the listener would get it correct? The tappers predicted 50%. What's interesting about this study is that out of a total of 120 songs, the listeners were only able to guess 3 of the 120 songs, or 2.5%. That's a big disconnect between 50% and 2.5%. Why? The problem is that when the tappers tapped, they were hearing the song in their head. For the listener, however, all they heard was a bunch of disconnected taps. It was like hearing Morse code. That's the curse of knowledge: The tapper knows the song and cannot imagine what it's like to lack that knowledge. Is this scenario not played out in enterprise sales every day when the salesperson cannot understand why buyers are so stupid that they cannot understand why they should buy? Although it took six months for salespeople to internalize their product, for example, it's now difficult for them to remember what it was like not to have that knowledge. They are cursed with knowledge. So, the next time you are in a customer meeting, double check that you are not tapping.

Combining the lack of customer knowledge with the curse of knowledge, one easily understands why salespeople find it difficult to provide the context needed for buyers to internalize the value of the seller's product.

Insight scenarios, however, force the salesperson to talk about how real people solved real problems using the seller's product; they are, therefore, an effective antidote to the curse of knowledge. Salespeople employing insight scenarios sidestep engaging in a debate with the buyer, because they simply present a scenario and allow the buyer to form their own conclusion. This approach allows salespeople to avoid engaging in conflict with a much more knowledgeable adversary.

Virtual test drive

You may wonder, would it not it be easier to just hit the customer between the eyes with your facts and figures instead of delivering them through insight scenarios? The problem is that facts and figures are too abstract. You cannot see them or feel them, so they do not feel like they affect you. Without context, facts and figures still leave the customer trying to figure out why it makes sense to buy, or even care.

The most important reason to make your sales message concrete is to let the buyer experience it personally. Studies have proven, for instance, that a story activates the region of the brain that processes sights, sounds, tastes, and movement.[15] Thus, a salesperson can share a story with a customer, and due to the transportation effect of story, it feels real. It's as if the customer took the salesperson's offering out for a virtual test drive. Contrast this approach to a salesperson delivering a factual data dump in the form of an 85-slide power point presentation.

---

[15]   PhysOrg.com, "Readers Build Vivid Mental Simulations of Narrative Situations, Brain Scans Suggest," 2009.

CHAPTER NINE

EMOTIONS

Over time rationality has come to define us as human beings, but rationality often conflicts with reality. Salespeople, for instance, know that the excessive use of facts can flood buyers with too much information, and result in paralysis for analysis. Salespeople also know that every great leader, Winston Churchill, JFK, Steve Jobs, and Warren Buffet, have used stories to inspire people to act, because people are seldom inspired by reason alone. When was the last time that you saw someone march on Washington because of charts, graphs, and bullet points?

Until recently, we could only guess as to what really inspires customers to buy, because the mind was inaccessible. Now, however, modern neuroscience has broken open the black box of our minds. We now have the tools, such as magnetic resonance imaging (MRI) brain scans that tell us a great deal about how people's decisions are influenced. In fact, neuroscience is now able to prove that emotions not only do not get in the way of rational thinking, they are essential to decision making.

For example, in 1982, Elliot, a patient of neurologist Antonio Demasio had a brain tumor removed, and only the emotional part of his brain was affected. The conventional view of neuroscience at the time was that if our feelings kept us from making good decisions, then surely Elliot would be better off without his feelings. The outcome, however, was quite sad. Elliot would endlessly deliberate over irrelevant details like whether to use a black or blue pen. His paralysis for analysis was pathological.[16] The moral of the story for salespeople is that we need to not just sell to Spock or we'll end up in paralysis for analysis. We also need to sell to the emotional Captain Kirk if we wish our customer to become motivated to act.

Memorable

Because stories are facts wrapped up in context and delivered with emotion, they are more memorable. In fact, Jerome Bruner, a cognitive psychologist, said that a fact wrapped in a story is 22 times more memorable than the mere fact itself.

This claim is backed up by a scientific study conducted by Dr. James L. McGaugh, founder of the Center for the Neurobiology of Learning and Memory at the University of California (Irvine). Here he discovered that rats remembered better if he injected them with strychnine, a poison that simulated adrenaline. It only worked, however, if the injection occurred after the event to be remembered.

---

[16] Antonio Demasio, Descartes' Error: Emotion, reason, and the human brain, 2005, p. 43.

It may seem odd that your learning could be improved after the event, until this is put into an evolutionary context. Imagine early man stumbling upon a tiger emerging from a cave. As the man runs for safety, his body is pumping with adrenaline, and this helps him to better remember that cave, thereby increasing his chances of survival.[17] The amount of adrenaline released is dependent on the intensity of emotion and the level of surprise. This explains why almost everyone is able to remember where they were, and what they were doing, when they found out about 9/11. They were shocked that it could happen, and they were filled with intense emotions of empathy and fear.

Back-flip

Even if a seller persuades a buyer how great an offering is with facts, such persuasion has only an intellectual basis, and buyers are not inspired to act on reason alone. To buy, the customer must not only think it's right, but more important, it has to feel right. It's a committee sale to Mr. Logic and Mr. Intuitive. That's why an insight scenario is so effective, because it takes facts, and wraps them up in emotion.

I learned how important it is for an idea to feel right a few years ago when I wanted to learn to do a standing back-flip.

---

[17] Dr. James McGaugh. (1999). Basolateral Amygdala Is Involved in Modulating Consolidation of Memory for Classical Fear Conditioning. *The Journal of Neuroscience, 19*(15),6615–6622.

I just could not convince myself to do a flip without the security of my coach spotting me. Even though he'd say encouraging things like "The worst that will happen is that you'll land on your knees. Don't be such a wimp Michael. The floor is padded for crying out loud." But that did not help. I already intellectually knew that the risk reward ratio was in my favor, but it was not enough to overcome my fear of failure. You see, I was petrified of landing on my head, and breaking my neck.

Just like the thought of doing a back-flip made me fear that I could break my neck, could not the thought of buying your product also make customers fear that they'll lose their job?

To take on risk, do you not agree that it's not enough for the buyer to think it is right, but that it's also has to feel right? Even when a buyer is convinced rationally, can that buyer really be expected to vote against his feelings? When sellers only offer a rational argument to buy, the only thing that feels real for the buyer is the fear of change. That is why sellers need to tell buyers an insight scenario that makes change (buying) feel less risky than the status quo.

Rational decision myth busted

Your skepticism may be bubbling up at this point, and you may wonder if you really need to make the before and after picture of owning your product feel real. I had the same question. After working on Wall Street for 14 years, I always presented facts and figures to B2B buyers, because that was how I felt serious business people made decisions. This belief was backed by 2,500 years of conditioning, beginning with Plato's view that man is rational, and that it is our emotions that interfere with rational decisions. Recently, however, I had an experience that called this belief into question. Then, shortly thereafter, I was presented with a compelling study from neuroscience that also refuted this belief. So when these two events collided, the myth that buying decisions were strictly rational was busted. I now understood why customers get stuck in paralysis for analysis, and what I can do to help then to avoid it.

My experience began when I was about to make the most important buying decision of my life. My daughter, Isabelle, was leaving her small community school, and was off to grade seven in the city. I had to make sure I made the right decision, so that she would be on the right track to get into a good university. I created a selection matrix on Excel, and off I went to the school's open houses to make the optimal choice.

The problem I faced was that all the schools seemed the same. I felt nothing. I was stuck in analysis paralysis. When a good friend, Prof. Pete, asked me how it was going, I said, "I cannot decide. I've seen seven of the top private schools, and not one has inspired me." Pete suggested I check out Voice, a small performing arts school in the distillery district not far from my home. Although I did not see how an Arts school could help get my daughter into a good university, I agreed to go, because I respected Pete's opinion.

The next week Pete asked me how it went. "Terrible," I said. "Within 5-minutes of visiting the school, Issy and I both decided on Voice, because it felt right." "Sounds great," said Pete, "but why is that terrible?" "It's terrible because the school failed on every one of my criteria. The teaching was average, the sports facilities were poor, and yet we chose the school because it felt right. Does that make me a bad parent?" "No Michael," Pete said, "don't be so hard on yourself. Most of our decisions are made unconsciously." Because Pete is a professor of neuroscience, he cited a study as proof. In this study, subjects were given a puzzle to solve, and by monitoring their brain activity with an EEG, researchers were able to show that the puzzle was actually solved eight seconds before the subjects were conscious of solving it.[18] "So Michael," Pete said, "at the open house I'm sure your unconscious mind was processing all the time in the background, and when it decided, it communicated its decision to your conscious mind through the emotion of certainty that Voice was the right choice."

"Come on Pete," I said, "I'm not going to believe that I bet my daughter's future on a gut feeling. Sorry Pete, but after reflecting on my decision, I realized that I chose Voice because Issy would gain self-confidence from participating in the performing arts." "Really," Pete said, "you decided all that in just five minutes of visiting the school? Or, did your rational mind fabricate a reason, so that you'd have a consistent narrative to consciously justify your subconscious decision."

"Wow, Pete," I said. "That's a little too cerebral for me. In layman's terms, do you mean it's like you and your wife? She makes most of the decisions, and you pretend

---

[18]   The Economist – "Incognito: Conscious and unconscious thought" 16-04-09.

that you are in charge?" "Yes," Pete said, "exactly, and there is a fascinating study to back it up. The subjects, who had just had their right and left hemisphere of their brains severed in order to treat epilepsy, were well chosen, because they provided the opportunity for the researchers to trick the brain. Because the left hemisphere processes language, the right hemisphere was mute. Thus, it could no longer articulate what it saw to others, or even itself. The only way that the right hemisphere could communicate what it subconsciously saw was by pointing. So, when the subjects' right hemisphere was shown a picture of a snowy winter scene, they were asked to point to one of five cards that represented what they had just seen, and the right hemisphere correctly pointed to a shovel. But when asked to verbally explain their choice, the right hemisphere could not do it, so the left hemisphere had to step in. The problem was that the left hemisphere did not know the reason why, because it had not seen the snowy picture. But did it admit that it did not know the answer or say here's my best guess? No, instead it fabricated a rational reason, and shamelessly said 'Oh, that's easy. The shovel was chosen to clean out the chicken shed.'" The answer is not as bizarre as it initially appears, because the left hemisphere was previously shown a picture of a chicken foot. So, the left hemisphere connected the shovel to a chicken foot, and then fabricated the reason that the shovel was chosen was to clean out the chicken shed.[19] "So Michael," said Pete, "this study may explain why the reason you think you

---

[19]   Gazzaniga,MichaelS.,"TheSplitBrainRevisited,"ScientificAmerican, July 1998

chose Voice was really nothing more than your rational mind trying to consciously justify your unconscious decision."

"Aha, I get it" I said. And suddenly everything started to make sense to me. Intuitively, I'd always known that people often make decisions emotionally, and then justify them with logic. But I did not have the proof to back up this theory. Now I understood. The reason I could not look back on a decision and see it as exclusively unconscious was because the rational mind would always fill in the gap with a fabricated reason. Now that the myth of the rational buyer was busted, I would forever change how I sold to B2B customers.

"And then he told a story, and everything changed."

Just last summer, I learned again how memorable facts are when they are wrapped in emotion.

As I watched my son's soccer game in the rain, the clouds grew dark, and I heard thunder. "We are in a bad place if there's lightning," warned the CEO of Colgate.

"But we are right next to a tall light-post," I countered. "Yes" said Scott, "but it needs to be grounded; otherwise, lightning can travel horizontally, and then... we're toast."

Oh please, I lamented, not another overly cautious warning. As Scott droned on about the dangers of lightning, I drifted away, and thought that Scott may know a lot about toothpaste, but meteorology... I do not think so.

Then he told a story, and everything changed. He recounted how he, three friends, and four caddies were playing golf in Colombia. Like today, there was rain, but it was the lightning that forced them to seek refuge inside a nearby kiosk. Inside, one of the caddies sat down on a metal box full of ice cold drinks, and sipped a Coca-Cola. Suddenly, lightning struck a tree 20 yards away, traveled horizontally, and then hit the metal box.

"Oh no, was the Caddy OK?" I asked. "No," Scott said, "he died."

"That's terrible; did you see it happen?" Scott looked down at the ground, paused, and then slowly responded in a quiet voice, "Yes, and he was just a child."

Scott then explained the dangers of lightning, and this time, I actually listened.

In fact, I'll never forget this story, and the poor boy that died. I'll also always remember that lightning can travel horizontally.

Part Three

How to create and deliver
Insight Scenarios

CHAPTER TEN

HOW TO CREATE INSIGHT SCENARIOS

I n this chapter, you are going to learn the seven steps to creating an insight scenario.

You may be thinking that this looks like a lot of work. Why bother creating insight scenarios when you already have lots of case studies? Case studies and insight scenarios are not the same thing, they do not produce the same effects, and they are not used for the same purpose. Case studies are useful as proof late in the sales cycle, when customers are looking to justify their buying decisions. Early in the sales cycle, however, case studies are not useful for two reasons. The first reason is that case studies are a conversation- killing monologue that floods the buyer with too much information. The second reason is that they focus too much on the details of the solution, with not enough time being spent illuminating the hidden value in the solution.

Step One—Why?

Write down what you want the insight scenario to do. You do not need an insight scenario to sell everything. Think of an insight scenario as a flashlight that you use to illuminate hidden value. So think of where that value is hidden, and create an insight scenario to make it known. Why is the customer, for example, not buying your product today, and what would the buyer need to believe to buy your product?

To avoid telling boring insight scenarios, you need to break the buyer's pattern, and for your insight scenario to stick, the customer needs to form a new pattern with a new story where new choices make more sense. Think about yourself. You see data, you look for a pattern, and then you tell yourself a story so that you make sense of the pattern. The story then creates an emotion, and it's that emotion that causes you to act. We are always seeking the meaning behind patterns, because uncertainty and chaos terrifies us. If we cannot find the meaning behind a pattern, we will make one up. What if the pattern is known? We will discount it, right? Why? Because it is not useful. Without this filter, we would drown in information. So think about the pattern the customer needs to see to buy your product, and the pattern they believe today. And if there's a big enough gap, then your insight scenario will be insightful, and engaging.

Step two—Setting

Pick a goal for a particular title/job function, vertical, and capability. Now put this down on paper into a sentence along the lines of, "Let me tell you about Paul, the VP of Finance of a manufacturing company, who was looking to reduce inventory costs."

People do not care about companies: They care about people. You need the setting so that the buyer knows who the insight scenario is about, and what this person was looking to achieve.

Step three—Complication

The complication is the most important part of the insight scenario, and it is the main area where insight scenarios fall flat. The common fault is that sellers gloss over the complication, because they do not know the details. The seller, for example, is often only able to paint a superficial picture of the problem, for instance, that the customer's current system is prone to error or lacks timeliness. Without contrast, there is no value, and the buyer either decides not to buy and to live with the problem, or wants a discount because of an inability to imagine the full value.

As an insight scenario is a word picture, you've got to be specific to make it real. One of the most effective ways to help the buyer to see this picture is to use a simile, metaphor, or an analogy. In the cartoon below, for example, the cartoonist simply could have stated that mental health should be treated like a physical disease, but the message would probably be blocked by our prejudice. So, instead, the cartoonist showed what would happen if physical diseases were treated like mental illness. In one of the cartoons, the doctor says to the patient "I get that you have food poisoning and all, but you have to at least make an effort."

It has been my experience that companies are able to find metaphors only 25% of the time for their insight scenarios, but when they do, the payoff is worth the effort.

Figure 6. Helpful Advice

Make sure you only have one problem per story. Otherwise, you will flood the buyer with too much information. This is a common problem, and one I often commit myself. You think "this one problem is great, but if I add just one more it will be even better." Then, suddenly, you have five or six problems in your story, and none of them stick.

Remember to wrap your facts in emotion; otherwise, the story will not stick. You've got to show how the people who populate your tale were affected to engage your audience.

The problem is that customers generally see themselves as okay, and not needing to change. That's the problem with most stories, because the seller just talks about how they helped the customer. Of course, we see what we want to see until we do not see it. Without a fully developed complication, you are trying to sell a rescue boat to people who are only ankle deep in problems. It's no wonder that they keep clipping you at the knees with objections, because they have no skin in the game. What you need to do is fully develop the complication in your story, so that buyers suddenly realize that they are not ankle deep in problems at all, but are, in fact, drowning. Then and only then will they be ready to believe in the viability of your solution. Because to see the delta of your offering, someone has to recognize the gap between how something is currently being done and how it could be done with your product (see figure 7).

Figure 7. Rescue Boat Before & After

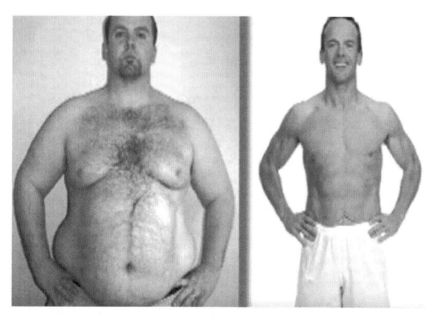

Figure 8. P-90x Before & After

No one shows the contrast I am talking about better than the exercise commercials P90X with the before and after picture. This is an insight scenario at its best. The complication is the before picture. You've got to have the fat guy in the before picture in order to sell the skinny guy, because the fat guy creates the contrast. More contrast creates more value. Thus, before you write your story, it is a good idea to draw it, to zero in, in other words, on a simple word picture that your story will clearly tell (see figure 9.)

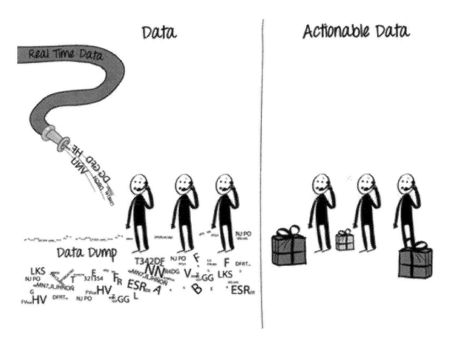

Figure 9. Data vs. Actionable Data

Step four—Villain

So many sellers' stories are about how they arrived as the hero on the white horse, and rescued the buyer. But the buyer does not want to see themselves as the loser in the story. Your story must attract, and not repel the buyer. You accomplish this by making the buyer the hero of the story.

Although every hero needs a villain, the villain cannot be buyer or their employees. Instead, make the villain an outside force such as changes in the status quo, economic times, market conditions, competitive landscape, technology, government regulation, etc.

Step Five—Turning Point

This is the "Aha!" moment when the buyers gain the insight that they must change. They finally realize that the cost of the status quo is greater than the cost of the seller's product plus the risk of change.

Step Six—Resolution

The resolution is the rescue. Be brief about describing how the buyer was rescued by your product, since you are just selling the concept in the story. You will prove it to the buyer later, going into the details about your solution once the buyer cares about the details. Do not describe what your offering is, because you may risk drowning the buyer in an overflow of information. Instead, describe how the buyer may use your offering to overcome the obstacles that are preventing them from achieving their goals. You may wish to quantify the value of the solution in general terms.

Step Seven—Questions

You only tell a story to hear the buyer's story. Your story helps buyers to find the "oil spills" in their own company. After you finish telling your story, say "that's enough about Paul, what's your story?" If your story does not resonate, move on to the next story. Buyers may need some help discovering their stories, and that is when you need to ask a few questions to help them qualify and quantify the cost of the status quo.

Write your own

Now you can create your own insight scenario with the template below. You want the story to be between 250 and 350 words so that you can deliver it in less than two minutes. Some people like to write it out, and others like to work from bullet points.

The best way to tell if you've written a memorable insight scenario is to tell it to a random salesperson, and see if they can repeat it back to you after hearing it only once. If your story is easy for your salespeople to deliver, then it will be easy for the customer to remember long after the details of your presentation have been forgotten.

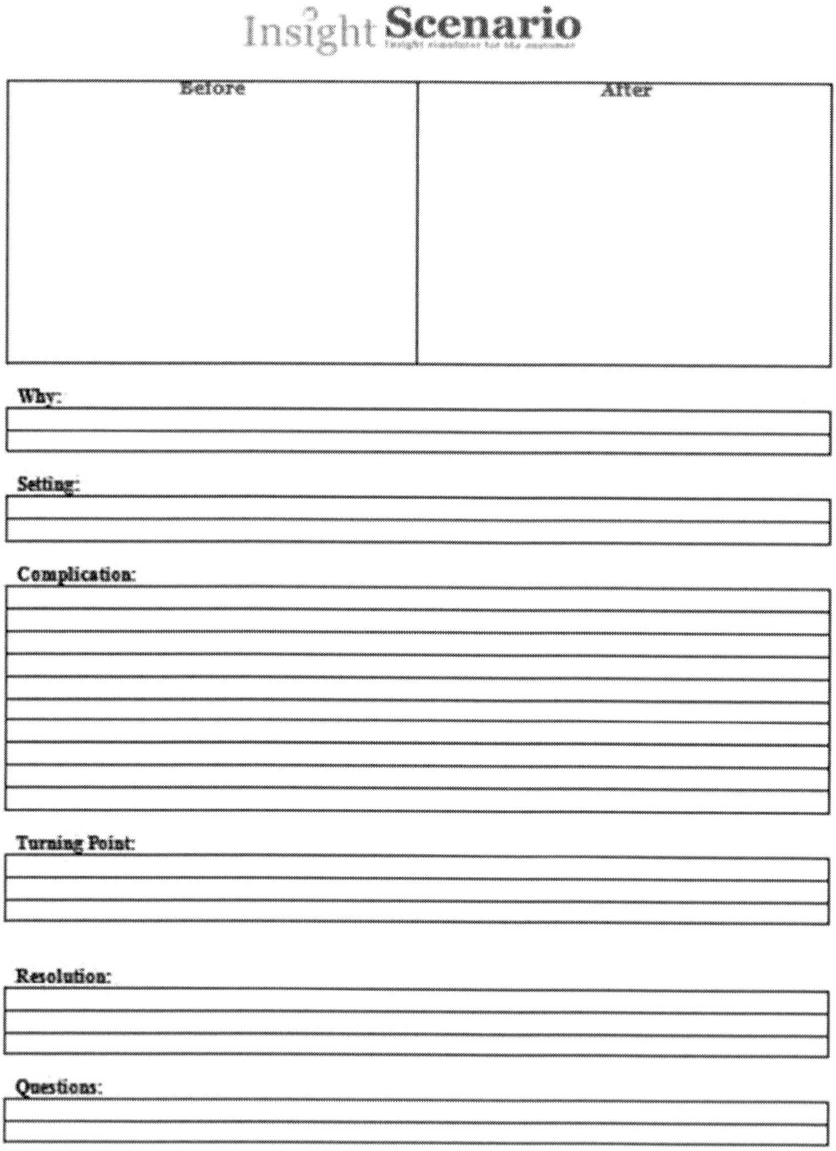

Insight **Scenario**

Before	After

Why:

Setting:

Complication:

Turning Point:

Resolution:

Questions:

Figure 10. Insight Scenario Template

Don't skip the details

When the best communicators seek to persuade, they provide just enough detail so that it feels like you stepped inside their idea simulator, and experienced it for yourself.

Now imagine if they had skipped the details. As you enter the idea simulator, you look around, and all you see is an empty white room devoid of details. And on a little white table, there is an index card with your five bullet points. And after reading the facts and figures contained in the five bullet points, you feel nothing, because you cannot see or feel facts and figures. They are just abstract concepts, because they do not feel like the affect you either directly or indirectly.

So next time you are trying to persuade someone, do not forget to add just enough detail, but not too much to cause overload.

Chapter Eleven

QUESTIONS

In a 45-minute customer meeting, a salesperson would only share two to four 2-minute insight scenarios. The other 80 to 90% of the meeting would be a dialogue between the buyer and the seller. That's why each insight scenario ends with "that's enough about client X, what's your story?"

And if the customer's buying vision is not clear, the salesperson can use questions to help the buyer fill in the gaps so that it becomes crystal clear.

The objective of questions is to help the customer paint their own crystal clear version of the before and after picture.

Drilling for Pain

In the before picture, you are trying to help the customer to see the problems and costs to their operations in the absence of having your unique capabilities. By helping the buyers to look into their own company, they will be able to determine the financial impact of their problems. An effective question to achieve this goal when you are drilling for pain is to ask "and then what happens?" If the customer states, for example, that the firm's Excel spreadsheet does not accurately track rebates, the salesperson could then ask "and then what happens?" The salesperson can then exchange this for "what's the impact?" or "and what's the consequence?" Once the salesperson asks this question a few times, the two of them get to the root cause of the problem, and the before picture will emerge with greater clarity. If the salesperson stops at the first question, they may not have created enough contrast. If the salesperson is not able to create contrast, then the buyer will not see value.

Once the salesperson has reached the root cause of the problem, the salesperson can then ask a few questions to determine the financial impact of the problem, or the cost of doing nothing about it. These questions should be worked out in advance of the meeting, because in my experience it is too difficult to create them on the fly. Salespeople should use the most simplistic back-of-the-envelope math; otherwise, the salesperson is going to be asking questions of the buyer that the buyer will not be able to answer.

Drilling for Gain

Sometimes buyers are looking to move towards a future destination as opposed to moving away from a problem. They will use phrases such as "our goal is to..." or "we are looking to...." At times like these, you are trying to help the customer paint their own vision of how much better off they would be if they own your product.

An effective question to ask when you are drilling for gain is "what would that allow you to do?" If the customer states that their Excel spreadsheets would accurately track rebates, for example, the salesperson could ask "if you could accurately track rebates, what would that allow you to do?" The salesperson can ask this question several times as a follow-up until there are no remaining blurs in the after picture.

Back of the Envelope

Some salespeople feel uncomfortable with back-of-the-envelope math, because they think it will appear amateurish to the Buyer. Without a background in finance, outsiders to finance tend to view the subject as akin to wizardry. But after working on Wall Street for 14 years with a graduate degree in finance, I have learned that finance is mostly made up of educated guesses. When valuing an investment, for instance, you will have to guess what will be the future income stream over the next five to 10 years. You'll then have to guess what will be the expenses. Once you subtract the projected expenses from revenue, you have your guestimate of what will be the before tax profit. You then need to know what is the present value of the future profit stream? That again requires another guesstimate for the discount rate. Once you've calculated the net present value, you have a way of converting all of your guesswork into a common language of money. This will allow you to compare one investment with another. That's what you are doing with back-of-the-envelope math. The seller, for example, helps the buyer to determine the cost of the problem versus the cost of the solution plus the risk of change. If the delta is great enough, the buyer will invest in the seller's product before other investments that have to be made. A cynic may say that even if the net present value is not high enough, it is easy for management to massage the guesstimates to produce the desired results.

What happens if the seller feels that it is too much work to help the buyer to quantify the value of the seller's product? Well, imagine that the buyer opens their desk drawer and looks at the seller's proposal that arrived yesterday via overnight mail. The buyer looks off into the distance, and reflects on the firm's problem. The seller did not have time to drill deep enough to reach the root cause, or to quantify the financial impact of the problem. So, as the buyer now reads the seller's proposal, the purchase price is shocking. Wow, $225,000 looks awfully big when the buyer compares it to a vague problem. So the buyer puts the proposal into the no decision today file, and decides to live with the problem.

Qualify

Sometimes it is difficult or inappropriate to quantify the impact of gain or pain. Some buyers, for example, are very intuitive, and they do not want to get dragged down into financial analysis. They know it's important, and they know they need to make a decision. Rarely in B2B sales is there only one decision-maker. So if you cannot quantify, at least try to qualify. Instead of drilling down to the financial impact, you can have the customer rate the importance of the problem or opportunity on a scale of 1 to 10. At least then, you will be able to qualify their belief, know how urgent it is, and what its priority is.

Chapter Twelve

LISTENING

Delivering insight through an insight scenario is not an end: It is simply a means to hearing the buyer's story. You only tell a story to hear the buyer's story. Hopefully your insight scenario will provide enough insight so that the buyer is able visualize a new story where new choices make more sense.

In a 45-minute customer meeting, for example, a salesperson may only share two to three two-minute insight scenarios. So the other 85% of the meeting is composed of listening and exploring the customer's situation. It's a dialog, not a monologue, and insight scenarios are like conversation starters. They ignite a conversation, because they are packed with insight.

Yes but...

As a salesperson, you want to know what the customer's buying vision is so that you can fill in the gaps with insight scenarios and questions. However, the customers' buying visions are like a movie that plays in their heads. The only way you will be able to see it is by listening. When you listen deeply to people, they listen to themselves, and sometimes that will be enough change their minds.

Most people think they listen, but they do not. Instead, they listen in order to make their point. Sure, there is active listening, but that is just externally going through the motions of listening. You look the buyer in the eye, pretend you are interested in what they are saying, and then repeat back to them what they have said. Really though you have just faked listening.

If the salesperson is thinking about making the sale while they listen to the buyer, for instance, the buyer will sense that the salesperson is only listening in order to impose an agenda. As a general rule, if buyers start to feel that their beliefs are being attacked, the conversation can quickly turn into a fight for control. The salesperson pushes out of fear of losing the sale, and the buyer pushes back out of fear of being manipulated.

To really listen to customers, the salespeople must think of their attention as a flashlight, and they must focus the light from themselves back onto the customer. To do this, salespeople must be completely present while they listen, and trust that they will know what to say when the buyer finishes speaking. Once the buyers feel that they have really been heard, they are able to go back to the place where they hide their uncertainties. Instead of telling their rehearsed stories, they are free to go back to the original data and tell themselves a new story that creates an emotion that then inspires them to act in new ways.

This is why an insight scenario is such an effective mechanism for delivering insight. The customer, for instance, will not be defensive when they listen to your story, because your story simply presents a scenario that allows the customer to draw their own conclusions. Without feeling pressured, the customer can now relax and listen to your message, and possibly gain enough insight that they start to formulate a new story, where new choices make more sense. And then, all the seller has to do is listen to the buyer's new story.

My lesson

I learned how effective listening can be 10 years ago when my family took a sabbatical in Argentina. It was there that my premature son was born. Before he was born, my wife was bedridden for three months with a low placenta. This gave me the opportunity to be with my daughter Isabelle full-time. Up until that time, my wife would always respond to Isabelle's needs a split second before I would. She is a great mother. When she was bedridden, however, I had Isabelle all to myself, and I was finally able to respond to her needs. For six months, we became an inseparable team. As soon as my son Max came back home from the hospital, however, Isabelle went right back to her mom. I was devastated. I can remember what my wife said: "Just get in her space Michael, and she'll come back to you." So that's what I did. I did not go to Isabelle with any agenda on what to do that day, or what we would do at that moment. All I would do was be 100% present with her, and listen to her without thinking what I'd say next. Sure enough, she came back to me. Is it any different with our business relationships? Think back to a time when you felt really heard in business? Did you feel a connection with that person? Did you trust them? Listening, in my opinion, is the least developed skill in sales, because we all think we do it. Listening is more than just listening to someone's words: It is listening without filters, or judgment. They say you are not really listening to people until you are willing to be changed by what they say.

Chapter Thirteen

EXAMPLES

Here are three examples of insight scenarios. We have also provided a before and after sample so that you will see the difference between an insight scenario that flops and one that pops.

Example One: "Improve customer churn"

Gabriella, the Manager of Customer Experience at Verizon, was looking for a faster way to implement Verizon's market research findings to improve the customer experience.

Although the quality of Verizon's market research was good, it took too long to be deployed because there was an 8-week delay to know, for instance, what Verizon's current customer service ratings were. In the fast-paced mobile technology sector, a customer could be long gone before the Market Research Department's well intended, but stale, business process changes took effect.

The CEO always said that the customer service ratings of Verizon's call agents were an early indicator of revenue trends. Thus, unless Market Research could operate with current data, it's initiatives to reverse the company's declining market share would be wasted.

That's why the CEO told Gabriella she had until the end of the quarter to find a solution.

The obvious choice was for Gabriella to just pick a cross channel customer experience system company that offered real time data from one of their existing channel providers.

Although having real time data was great, what Gabriella really needed, and what the three providers could not offer, was the ability to immediately funnel the real time data back to the front-lines call center agents. The agents needed more than standardised data, they needed individualized data that applied immediately to their jobs. Gabriella knew the call agents would not look through a 300-page real time data report. They would only read one page as long as it applied to them and what they could do to improve.

Fortunately, Gabriella was referred to CEM Corp by the end of quarter deadline. By implementing CEM Corp's capabilities, Verizon was able to increase the overall customer experience scores by 6% in the first 30 days. The CEO was right. Improving customer experience helped reverse the firm's declining market share.

But that's Gabriella's story, what's your story?

Example Two: "Age plus"

John Allen, Director of Water and Environment for a well known city, was looking to reduce operating costs. The problem was that his actuals were much higher than the estimated budget, and he could not understand why.

Although there were an abnormal number of service request calls, without a way to see a trend, John needed to investigate why. The answer came from his crew supervisor, who reported that most of these complaints were coming from a new subdivision. John thought that was very odd since the pipes were almost new. An onsite investigation revealed that the cause of the problem was the PVC piping. Under normal circumstances, PVC was fine. However, in this subdivision the acidic soil in the area had prematurely corroded the PVC pipe. So, by using PVC pipe instead of cast iron, the expected life of the pipe was reduced from 60 to six years. This unforeseeable problem had increased their costs by over 10 times.

Because there may be other areas in the city with the same issues, John decided to put together a team to investigate how they could pinpoint other problem areas.

The team discovered Geospatial Corp. Geospatial Corp highlighted that only tracking the age of the pipe was limiting the team's ability to maximize the life of their assets.

By aggregating all of the data from CAD mapping, Oracle WAM, Soil Type, Geospatial Corp was able to check whether there were other areas with acidic soil where PVC pipes should be replaced with cast iron.

The team discovered two other areas, and displayed them on a map using hot spot analysis. This discovery resulted in millions of dollars in savings and fewer service request calls.

Aside from overlaying acidic soil, John's team is also able to see how traffic, weather, and many other variables may impact the expected age of the pipes.

But that's John's story; what's yours?

Example Three: "Truly profitable orders"

Maxine, the Supply Chain Director of Asahi Glass, wanted a way to know what orders were truly profitable.

Up until now, the salespeople had been using a static snapshot of profitability.

Maxine, however, was disappointed to see profitable deals later become money losers, because the salespeople would place orders with no insight into how they impacted current capacity, nor if their rush order would negatively impact other orders.

Maxine needed to find a way to have a more dynamic view of profitability. Something that was simple for the salespeople to use. What she envisioned was something as simple as booking a flight online; with a number of scheduling options according to price for the customer, and true profitability for Maxine's company.

Maxine finally had enough when a salesperson's profitable Toyota order quickly turned into a substantial money loser, because her company was forced to fly parts into the plant to avoid delayed order penalties.

Fortunately, the Toyota order inspired Maxine to look for a solution, and she found more than what she was looking for with Advance Schedule Corp.

We provided Maxine with the ability to see each potential order's impact on capacity, and then how it affected other orders.

But the sales team was over the moon that they could now do sales campaigns by pooling their orders along with price incentives, so that they could not just generate more sales, but more important, maintain profitability.

But that's Maxine's story, what's yours?

Flops vs. Pops

By recognizing the difference between an insight scenario that "pops" versus one that "flops," you can see for yourself how your own insight scenarios can be changed so that they inspire prospective customers to buy, instead of providing them with no reason to change.

The mistakes made in the story that flops are common. Because the effects of not having the seller's capabilities are abstract, the story fails to make the buyer want to change, because the risks do not feel real.

As Anthony Wallace, Director of Asia Pacific and Japan CA Technologies, said:

> As Story 1 (flops) is all about the facts – it is not personal, you do not gain a sense of the contrast between the pain and the gain. Story 2 (pops) is personal – it's told through the lens of Rob and the challenge he was facing. The anecdote about the toll bridge is concrete, conjuring up the image of potholes in the road and placing 20,000 pins on a map is concrete. This form of rational drowning

can trigger emotion as does the quantified gains
– one click, 25% reduction in 18 months.

So, look at the story that pops and the story that flops, and see which story one of your salespeople could repeat back to you after hearing it only once. If these insight scenarios are easy for your salespeople to deliver, then they will be easy for your customers to remember long after the details of your presentation have been forgotten.

1- Example of an insight scenario that flops

Rob Jones, Deputy Manager of Operations for the City of Allentown, PA was looking at innovative ways to increase productivity and create efficiencies in all their business processes. To do this he wanted to coordinate work with his Engineering Land Development Department to optimize resources and improve his operational budget by reducing service requests.

Using technology and workflows available to the City, temp staff was hired to review work orders and service requests and place pins on a map to illustrate where problems occurred. This was a lengthy and resource intensive process that delayed capital improvement planning (CIP) for Engineering. With the growth of the City and increased demands placed on limited City resources, something had to change.

Using a Geo-centric approach to managing and maintaining all infrastructure assets, City Operations decided to implement GISworks. Capital Engineering was also experiencing problematic workflows due to the fast paced growth and change within the City.

Once implemented and the history began to compile within GISworks, Capital Engineering was able to leverage historical maintenance data/history from the system to help make better decisions with regards to long term, sustainable capital planning. They did this by using Geospatial Corp's GIS to overlay all WO and SR from GISworks with the CIP for more accurate and realistic analysis.

Rob Jones stated that while workflow issues between operations and capital planning groups are not uncommon in local government organizations, in Surrey, these two often disparate thinking groups where brought together through the use of this software. Both groups now have a far better understanding and appreciation of how their decisions impact the entire system at a high level.

2- Example of a story that pops.

Rob Jones, Deputy Manager of Operations for the City of Allentown, was looking to reduce the number of service requests by 25%.

The problem was that he had the same level of staff that he had 15 years ago, but the infrastructure that they managed had doubled. As a result, they were now only able to handle 75% of the service requests.

Because the Engineering Land Development and the Capital Engineering departments were already very efficient, Rob felt that they would need new tools if they were going to further reduce the service requests.

This became apparent to Rob when a new toll was put on the city bridge. Instead of paying the toll, the truckers diverted through the city streets. Because the city streets were not designed to handle the increased traffic and weight of the trucks, there was a surge in pothole service requests.

Although Capital Engineering could not possibly have planned for this, Rob felt that if they had a new tool that would have allowed them to overlay their service requests onto a map, then they could have been alerted early to the trucker's new route. With this new information, Capital Engineering could have altered their capital plan to reinforce the road before it was damaged, and before the surge in pothole service requests.

Rob could have hired temporary staff to place pins on a map to illustrate where the service requests were occurring. However, transferring 20,000 service requests onto a map with pins would have taken months, and even worse, the data could have been up to 12 months old. Because of these delays, the changes to the capital plan would have occurred after the road was already damaged, and after the surge in pothole service requests.

So, Rob concluded that with the ability of GISworks to overlay service requests onto the capital plan with the click of a button, they could not only optimize their plans for roads, but also for water-mains and sewers. Within 18 months of using GISworks, Rob's team was able to reduce the number of service requests by 25%.

But that's Rob's story, what's yours?

CHAPTER FOURTEEN

COACHING

Without a helicopter view of the customer's world, salespeople are selling blind. When they do stumble across a customer's pain point, they can only refer to vague pain points (i.e., "time consuming" or "prone to error"), because their knowledge of the customer is superficial. The result is that too many salespeople are trying to rescue customers that are only ankle deep in problems. No wonder over 60% of sales opportunities end with the customer deciding to do nothing.

You can coach your Reps with stories to find and then fill customer knowledge gaps in just 10-minutes a week. Because stories present a clear before and after picture of owning your product, knowledge gaps are immediately exposed when the picture is out of focus.

Increase Value & Win More Sales

Once Reps learn how to fill the gaps, their ability to sell value will explode. They will learn, for example, that as they crank up the contrast between the before and after picture of the customer owning their product, they also crank up the value of their product in the customer's eyes. That is when the magic happens. It is the contrast that creates the spark for the customer that ignites the Reps' sales process.

This type of sales coaching is made by your salespeople for your salespeople. They will learn by doing, and then by observing their peers. This is the same process that Toastmasters has used to train over 4 million people since 1924.

Studies show that the benefits of sales coaching are not fuzzy; they are overwhelming. In CSO Insight's 2013 study of 4,500 companies, for example, they discovered that companies that had a defined versus an ad hoc system for sales coaching were:[20]

- Two times more likely to be a trusted adviser versus just an approved vendor.
- +17% more hit sales quota.
- +24% more forecast deals won.

Here's how it works

At every sales meeting, your Reps will decide what they feel is the most pressing challenge their customers face. You will then assign a Rep to deliver a two-minute story

---

[20] www.csoinsights.com/Publications/Shop/sales-management-optimization

on this topic at the next sales meeting. This should take the Rep less than an hour.

After the Rep delivers the story, you will assign different Reps to act as Story Coaches. They will evaluate the story and provide positive and constructive feed-back on the following criteria:

- Are you a buyer?
- Is the story memorable?
- Is the contrast clear between the before and after?
- Did they drill down to the tangible impact of the customer's pain points?
- Was the insight scenario too long? (more than 2 min. or 250-350 words), and
- Were you lost? (more than 1 point).

Based on the feedback, the Rep edits the story, writes it up, and publishes it so that your team will have a valuable sales asset to use to help win future sales opportunities.

Just like Toastmasters, your Reps will learn by doing. They will also learn from observing their peers tell their stories. So by doing and observing, they will discover for themselves why some insight scenarios pop and others flop.

The Reps will then be able to take these bite-sized customer insights and deliver them in a short effective insight scenario, so that customers may start to tell themselves a new story where new choices make more sense. At every sales meeting, your Reps will decide what they feel is the most pressing challenge their customers face.

Conclusion

All salespeople want to be viewed as trusted advisors, but there are no short cuts. It is more than following a sales process. Salespeople need the customer knowledge to be granted permission to go from step to step. Buyers need a wise guide, one who can lead them through all of the information and advice that is available on the Internet.

Even though that is what buyers need, it may not be what they initially want. By the time buyers engage with a salesperson, they may already have an idea of their needs, the solution they believe they want, and what they are willing to pay. So how does the seller use insight to challenge the customer's thinking without challenging the customer?

We discussed how when it comes to resistant problems, verbal persuasion rarely works. It can come across as an attack, and make the buyer feel badgered or manipulated. When the seller illuminates a challenge with insight, the buyer does not merely believe the seller is wrong; the buyer needs for the seller to be wrong to protect the status quo. The last thing an overwhelmed buyer needs is to invest time into a problem they do not fully understood, and then buy a complex solution that is not only expensive but could also end up getting them fired.

But the instant the seller stops trying to impose their agenda on the buyer, the seller eliminates the fight for control, and the seller's insights are more likely to reach past the customer's defensive wall. Insight scenarios exert extraordinary influence because they transport the buyer out of the role of critic, and into the role of participant. Insight scenarios do not merely trump verbal persuasion by disproving counterarguments; they keep the buyer from offering counter arguments in the first place.

If your salespeople shared just one insight scenario per meeting, and did everything else the same, would customers relate more to what your salespeople are selling? Would you sell more?

INDEX

ABOUT THE AUTHOR

As CEO of Insight Demand, I enjoy showing salespeople how to find, create, and deliver insights so that they are able to sell value and differentiate their product.

With a graduate degree in Finance and 12 years of Wall Street experience, I learned how to build business value. I then ran a finance company that grew to 125 employees and 250MM sales, and it was here I learned the power of loading the lips of your salespeople with the right messages. I then worked as a Business Partner at a Solution Selling Sales Training company and, after five years, I refined the totality of my many years of experience and formed Insight Demand.

I have lived & worked in NYC, London and Buenos Aires. Today, I live on an Island with no cars that is only 10-minutes by ferry to my hometown, Toronto. I still travel to the big cities on business, but I am also able to enjoy Kite Surfing, Surfing and Hockey 20-meters from my home. I enjoy these simple pleasures with my wife and two children.

Workshops & Speaking

Workshops

2-day Insight Selling Workshop-learn by doing.

Unlike many training programs that become shelf-ware at the end of the workshop, your salespeople will have 6-8 Insight Scenarios that they can immediately share with customers to win more business.

If your salespeople shared just one story per meeting, and changed no other behavior, would customers relate more to what your salespeople are selling? Could your salespeople sell more?

Keynote Speaking

Michael Harris will show your salespeople how how to inspire customers to buy with Insight Selling.

Because insight scenarios help customers to realize that they are rationally and emotionally drowning in problems, your salespeople will finally be able to rescue more customers with your product.

Contact www.InsightDemand.com for more details.

INSIGHT DEMAND

We are an Insight Selling sales training company.

We show salespeople how to find, create, and deliver insights so that they are able to sell value and differentiate their product.

Through a combination of insight scenarios™, listening, and questions, customers will realize that they're not ankle deep in problems, but that they're really drowning out in the middle of the lake. The result is that your salespeople will sell more, because they will be able to rescue more customers with your product.

Our clients include such companies as Microsoft, Epicor Software, Eaton Corp, Hitachi, and Transunion Corp (see testimonials video).

We service clients in North America, Europe, and Asia.

www.InsightDemand.com